What is it made from?

Bobbie Kalman

🌿 Crabtree Publishing Company
www.crabtreebooks.com

Created by Bobbie Kalman

Author and Editor-in-Chief
Bobbie Kalman

Educational consultants
Elaine Hurst
Joan King
Jennifer King

Notes for adults
Jennifer King

Editors
Kathy Middleton
Crystal Sikkens

Design
Bobbie Kalman
Katherine Berti

Print and production coordinator
Katherine Berti

Prepress technician
Katherine Berti

Photo research
Bobbie Kalman

Photographs by Shutterstock

Library and Archives Canada Cataloguing in Publication

Kalman, Bobbie, 1947-
      What is it made from? / Bobbie Kalman.

(My world)
Issued also in electronic format.
ISBN 978-0-7787-9562-9 (bound).--ISBN 978-0-7787-9587-2 (pbk.)

      1. Materials--Juvenile literature. I. Title. II. Series: My world
(St. Catharines, Ont.)

TA403.2.K34 2011   j620.1'1   C2010-907442-4

Library of Congress Cataloging-in-Publication Data

Kalman, Bobbie.
  What is it made from? / Bobbie Kalman.
       p. cm. -- (My world)
  ISBN 978-0-7787-9587-2 (pbk. : alk. paper) -- ISBN 978-0-7787-9562-9
(reinforced library binding : alk. paper) -- ISBN 978-1-4271-9669-9
(electronic (pdf))
  1. Materials--Juvenile literature. I. Title.
  TA403.2.K34 2011
  620.1'1--dc22
                                                        2010047638

Crabtree Publishing Company

www.crabtreebooks.com   1-800-387-7650

Printed in China/022011/RG20101116

Published in Canada
Crabtree Publishing
616 Welland Ave.
St. Catharines, Ontario
L2M 5V6

Published in the United States
Crabtree Publishing
PMB 59051
350 Fifth Avenue, 59th Floor
New York, New York 10118

Published in the United Kingdom
Crabtree Publishing
Maritime House
Basin Road North, Hove
BN41 1WR

Published in Australia
Crabtree Publishing
386 Mt. Alexander Rd.
Ascot Vale (Melbourne)
VIC 3032

Words to know

wood

binoculars   furniture   glass   materials

object

paper

sand

sap

rubber   metal

tire

weight

wool

3

Objects are things we can see and touch.
They can look and feel different.
Objects are made from **materials**.
Paper, wood, glass, rubber, and metal
are some materials.

sweater
(wool)

book
(paper)

chair
(wood)

car
(glass,
metal,
rubber)

This boy is lifting a **weight**.
Weights are made of **metal**.
Metal is a hard material.
It comes from the ground.
These objects are made
of metal.

pot

weight

keys

lock

Some **furniture** is made of **wood**.

These beds are made of wood.

Where does wood come from?

Wood comes from trees.
What else comes
from trees?
Did you guess **paper**?

Books are made
of paper.
Find five objects
in your home
that are made
of wood or paper.

binoculars

The boy is looking through **binoculars**.

He sees many windows.

Windows are made of **glass**.

His binoculars also have glass in them.

The boy can see through the glass.

Many objects are
made of glass.
The girl is holding
a glass of orange juice.
The boy is
wearing glasses.
Do you know where
glass comes from?
It comes from **sand**!

sand

Do you wear **rubber** boots
when it rains?
Rubber boots
keep your feet dry.
Does your bike have
rubber **tires**?

rubber tires

rubber boots

10

Did you know that rubber comes from rubber trees? It is made from **sap** inside the trees. Sap is a white liquid that looks like milk.

pail

sap

11

Wool is a soft material.

It keeps you warm when it is cold.

Do you wear sweaters, hats,

and gloves made of wool?

sweater

hat

gloves

wool

Did you know that
wool comes from the
coats of sheep?
This lamb's wool coat
is being **sheared**,
or cut off.

wool

Activity

Which objects are made
of these materials?

1. wood
2. metal
3. wool
4. glass
5. rubber

(c)

(d)

(e)

15

Notes for adults

Objectives
- to teach children what many familiar objects are made from
- to teach children the raw materials used to make familiar objects
- to introduce the words "objects" and "materials" and allow children to explore how familiar things are made

Before reading
Write these six words on the board: wool, paper, wood, glass, metal, rubber
Ask the children to walk around the room to find objects made of these materials (desks, books, writing paper, toys, teaching aids, windows).
Ask the children:
"What is it made from?"
"Could it be made from a plant?"
"How does it feel? Describe its texture."

Questions after reading the book
"What are objects?" (things we can see and touch, such as books)
"What materials are objects made of?" (wool, wood, paper, glass, metal, rubber)
"What is a sweater made of?" (wool)
"What is a book made of?" (paper)
"What is a desk made of?"(wood, metal)
"What is a car made of?" (glass, rubber, metal)

"Where does wool come from?" (sheep)
"Where does wood come from?" (trees)
"Where does paper come from?" (trees)
"Where does metal come from?" (the ground)
"Where does rubber come from?" (rubber-tree sap)
"Where does glass come from?" (sand)

Activity: Around the room!
Have the children take pre-cut cards with the different materials written on them and label objects around the room.
Example: The children can label the windows, doors, furniture, mirrors, books, art paper, and dress-up clothes.
Set up six centers with a chart at each center. Give each center a different theme: wool, paper, wood, glass, metal, and rubber. Have the children draw and label one or two items that belong in each center. Example: wool (mittens, sweater)

Extension: Scavenger Hunt!
Tell the children that they are going to work as detectives to find different objects and discover what they are made of and from. Take them on an outdoor walk around the school. Using disposable or digital cameras, ask them to take pictures of the different objects they have seen and find out what they were made of. Then probe further into the raw materials from which those objects were made. (A car tire is made of rubber; rubber comes from rubber-tree sap.)

For teacher's guide, go to www.crabtreebooks.com/teachersguides